Canadian Animals
Star-nosed Moles

Christine Webster

Weigl

Published by Weigl Educational Publishers Limited
6325 10th Street S.E.
Calgary, Alberta
T2H 2Z9

www.weigl.com
Canadian Animals series © 2011
Weigl Educational Publishers Limited

Library and Archives Canada Cataloguing in Publication
Webster, Christine
Star-nosed moles / Christine Weber.

(Canadian animals)
Includes index.
Issued also in electronic format.
ISBN 978-1-55388-665-5 (bound).–ISBN 978-1-55388-666-2 (pbk.)

1. Star-nosed mole–Canada–Juvenile literature.
I. Title. II. Series: Canadian animals (Calgary, Alta.)

QL737.I57W42 2010   j599.33'5   C2009-907373-0

Editor
Josh Skapin
Design
Terry Paulhus

Photograph Credits
Every reasonable effort has been made to trace ownership and to
obtain permission to reprint copyright material. The publishers would
be pleased to have any errors or omissions brought to their attention
so that they may be corrected in subsequent printings.

Weigl acknowledges Getty Images as its primary image supplier for
this title.
Amanda Hill: page 14; Alamy: page 21; W.T. Helfrich: pages 2, 3, 4;
Ottmar Bierwagen: page 6, page 13; Peter Kelly: page 12; Jon Hall
www.mammalwatching.com

We gratefully acknowledge the financial support of the Government of
Canada through the Canada Book Fund for our publishing activities.

Printed in United States of America in North Mankato, Minnesota
1 2 3 4 5 6 7 8 9 0 14 13 12 11 10

072010
WEP230610

Contents

Meet the Star-nosed Mole

Star-nosed moles are small mammals with a special nose. Fleshy, finger-like **tentacles** flare out from the nose. These tentacles are sensors, or feelers, that help star-nosed moles find food.

Star-nosed moles are about 17.5 to 20.5 centimetres long. This is half the size of a small cat. Star-nosed moles have a tail that is about 6.5 to 8.5 centimetres long.

▶ Star-nosed moles live three to four years in nature.

Star-Nosed Mole Facts

- There are 22 tentacles on the star-nosed mole's nose.

- The star-nosed mole does not **hibernate** in winter. It hunts in the icy waters near its home.

▲ The star-nosed mole's body is covered in coarse, dark fur.

A Very Special Animal

The star-nosed mole has poor eyesight. In fact, it is nearly blind. It uses its other senses to help it survive. The star-nosed mole may have the best sense of touch of any mammal. It uses its tentacles to quickly touch the ground around it. The star-nosed mole does this so fast, the movement cannot be seen by the human eye.

▲ Star-nosed moles have strong hearing and can smell scents from a great distance.

The star-nosed mole can store fat in its tail. This makes the tail swell three to four times its normal size.

The nose is hairless and has two nostrils.

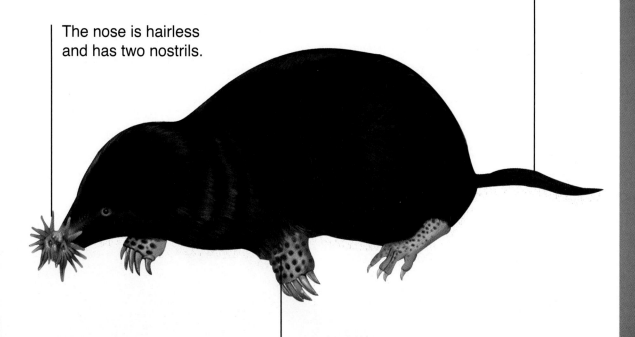

The star-nosed mole's strong legs are used for swimming.

Where Do They Live?

The star-nosed mole lives in Canada and the United States. It has a **range** of about 4,000 square metres.

It is rare for people to see star-nosed moles in nature. This is because these animals live beneath the ground. They **burrow** in moist soils near water. The areas where star-nosed moles live are called wetlands. The star-nosed mole makes its nest in a dry area of its burrow. Nests are made from dry leaves or grass.

▼ There are many kinds of moles. Like the star-nosed mole, all kinds of moles dig tunnels to look for food.

Star-nosed Mole Range

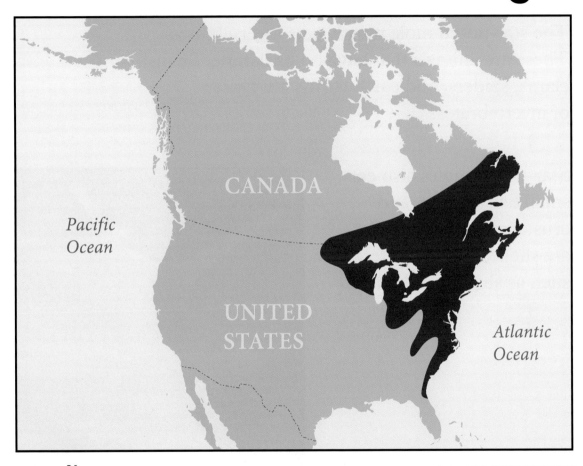

CANADA

Pacific
Ocean

UNITED
STATES

Atlantic
Ocean

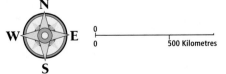

0
0
500 Kilometres

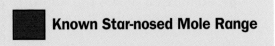

Known Star-nosed Mole Range

What Do They Eat?

The star-nosed mole mostly eats invertebrates. These are animals that have no backbone. Snails, clams, spiders, and earthworms are types of invertebrates.

Star-nosed moles also eat small fish, insects, and crustaceans. Crustaceans are shelled invertebrates, such as shrimp and crabs.

▶ Star-nosed moles are known to eat snails.

What a Meal!

Scientists have found that the star-nosed mole can eat 10 chunks of earthworm, one at a time, in 2.3 seconds.

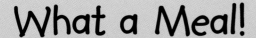

▼ Earthworms make up 90 percent of the star-nosed mole's diet.

Making Friends

Star-nosed moles form small **colonies**. These colonies work together to build tunnels. Male and female star-nosed moles share tunnels during mating season. Male and female star-nosed moles stay together until their young are born.

▼ Star-nosed moles hunt on their own. They start doing this when they are about three weeks old.

Star-nosed Mole Talk

Star-nosed moles make a high-pitched squeal when they feel threatened. They also use scent markings to communicate. Scent markings are odours left on plants by animals rubbing against them.

▲ The star-nosed mole sometimes makes a wheezing sound.

Growing Up

A star-nosed mole can have babies of its own by 10 months of age. Females carry the babies for 45 days. Female moles give birth in late spring. A mole has one **litter** each year. Most litters have two to seven babies.

Star-nosed mole babies are hairless and pink. At two weeks of age, they begin using their senses to guide them.

▼ Star-nosed mole's eyes and ears remain closed until 14 days after birth.

▶ An adult
star-nosed mole
weighs about
71 grams.

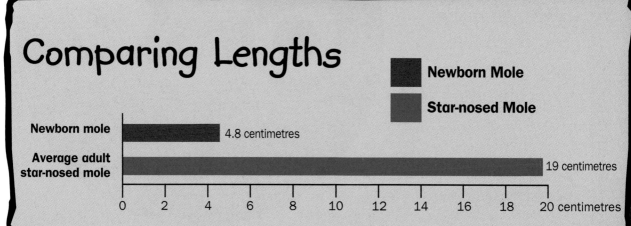

Comparing Lengths

■ Newborn Mole

■ Star-nosed Mole

Newborn mole — 4.8 centimetres

Average adult star-nosed mole — 19 centimetres

0 2 4 6 8 10 12 14 16 18 20 centimetres

Enemies

Like most animals, the star-nosed mole has enemies. Common **predators** include hawks, large fish, skunks, and even cats and dogs. Humans are also enemies to the star-nosed mole.

The star-nosed mole can be a pest to humans. Sometimes, these animals dig tunnels to travel under lawns. Humans may trap moles to keep them from damaging their yard.

▶ Owls are known to hunt the star-nosed mole.

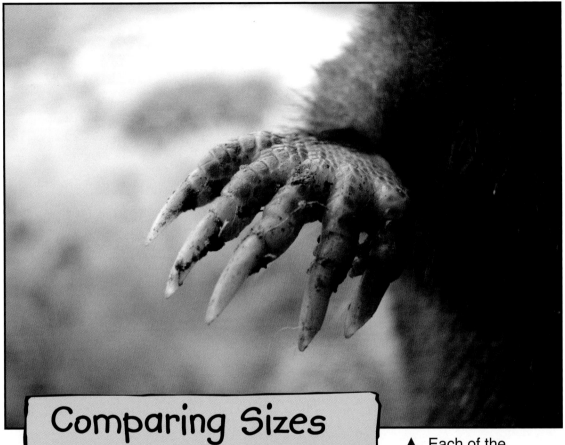

Comparing Sizes

The star-nosed mole can build tunnels as deep as 270 metres. This is the same as four and a half hockey rinks.

▲ Each of the star-nosed mole's toes has a sharp claw that is used to dig tunnels.

Under Threat

People build homes and businesses in wetland areas. This is a threat to the star-nosed mole. Construction destroys the star-nosed mole's habitat. As more of its habitat is destroyed, there are fewer places for the star-nosed mole to live. The animals star-nosed moles eat also live in wetlands. Construction threatens these animals, leaving less for star-nosed moles to eat.

▼ Fourteen percent of Canada is covered in wetlands.

What Do You Think?

The star-nosed mole depends on its wetland habitat for food and shelter. Humans have destroyed many wetlands for development. This may hurt the star-nosed mole population. Should development in wetlands be allowed? Should it be stopped to save wetland animals?

▲ In some parts of Canada, 70 percent of wetlands have been destroyed.

Myths and Legends

Moles have been in North America for more than 100 million years. It is believed moles lived in Europe even earlier.

▼ Moles have been the subject of stories for hundreds of years.

Aboriginal Peoples tell a story that explains why moles live underground. The mole in the story helps a man marry a woman who does not love him. When the woman is asleep, the mole steals her heart and brings it to the man. The man then swallows the woman's heart. When the woman awakes, she is in love with the man. Those who know the man and woman are angry at the mole for tricking the woman. The mole hides under the earth. Moles have lived underground ever since.

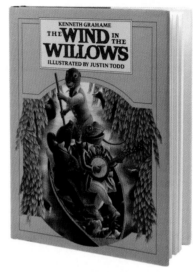

▲ *The Wind in the Willows* is a popular children's book. One of its main characters is a mole.

The star-nosed mole has been used as a character in movies and television shows. The Walt Disney film *G-Force* has a star-nosed mole named Speckles as one of its heroes. Actor Nicolas Cage is the voice of Speckles in the film.

Quiz

1. Where does the star-nosed mole live?
   (*a*) **North America** (*b*) **China** (*c*) **Europe**

2. How many babies does the star-nosed mole have each year?
   (*a*) **1 to 2** (*b*) **2 to 7** (*c*) **none**

3. What are a star-nosed mole's tentacles used for?
   (*a*) **sensors** (*b*) **decoration** (*c*) **climbing**

4. What do star-nosed moles eat?
   (*a*) **chickens**
   (*b*) **invertebrates**
   (*c*) **bullfrogs**

Answers:
1. (a) The star-nosed mole lives in North America.
2. (b) The star-nosed mole has 2 to 7 babies each year.
3. (a) The tentacles are used as sensors to detect food.
4. (b) They eat invertebrates, such as earthworms.

Find out More

To find out more about the star-nosed mole, visit the websites in this book.

College of Environmental Science and Forestry
www.esf.edu/aec/adks/mammals/starnosed_mole.htm

Nature History Notebooks
www.nature.ca/notebooks/english/starmole.htm

Benedictine University
www.ben.edu/museum/starnosed_mole.asp

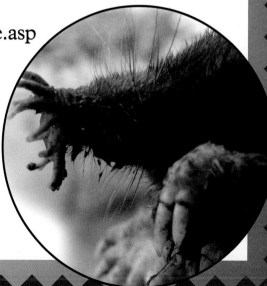

Words to Know

burrow
to dig a hole in the ground

colonies
groups of star-nosed moles that
live together

hibernate
to sleep through the winter

litter
a group of baby animals born at the
same time

predators
animals that hunt other animals for food

range
the land on which an animal lives
and hunts

tentacles
finger-like sensors that help animals
find food

Index